The P...

The puzzles in this book are based on
The New International Version
of The Bible

The Puzzling Book

Compiled by
Kirsti Paterson

Artwork by
Janis Mennie

Christian Focus Publications

Published by
Christian Focus Publications
Houston, Texas, U.S.A.   Tain, Ross-shire, Scotland

ISBN 0 906731-81-X
© 1988 Christian Focus Publications

Contents

Contents

Section 1

A Mixture of Matching

MATCHING

Match a name in one column with
their description in the other.

SOLOMON	FIRST WOMAN
ELISHA	DISCIPLE
EVE	KING
PETER	QUEEN
VASHTI	SPY
NICODEMUS	FIRST MAN
CALEB	RULER
ADAM	SOLDIER
POTIPHAR	PROPHET

Bible people who belong together.

~ Complete these pairs ~

Scribes and _____

Martha and _____

Ananias and _____

Aquila and _____

Sodom and _____

David and _____

Find the missing letters-1
A storm is calmed.

Read Mark 4 verses 35-41 and then fill in the missing letters in the story below.

At night J_s_s and his d__c_p-es went into a boat. Jesus had just finished speaking to a large crowd of p__p-e. At sea a str_ng w___ started. Big w____ broke over the b___. The disciples were a____d. Jesus was a____p in the stern. He was wakened by the disciples. They said "_e_____,don't you care if we d____?"
Jesus got up and said to the waves "Quiet! Be _____."
Everything was _____.

Picture Words

Use the first letter of each picture to find
a Bible message.

D r ch O ,

ee y u e ve

r do

Now write out the verse below:

____ _____, ____

_____ ___ _____.

1 o n 5 v. 21.

- Match the brothers -

Draw a line from a name on the left hand side to a name in the other column.

Abel	Jacob
Andrew	Moses
Esau	Joseph
Benjamin	Cain
Aaron	Naphtali
James	Japheth
Dan	John
Shem	Peter

In the right order

Write in the correct number for each. Then put them in the right order, 1 to 10, i.e. find answer 1 then 2 and so on····

1. The number of Gospels _____
2. The number of times Peter denied Jesus _____
3. The number of sheep who were lost out of the hundred _____
4. The number of chapters in I Timothy _____
5. The number of sons of Jesse _____
6. The number of commandments God gave to Moses. _____
7. The number of sisters of Lazarus _____
8. The number of lepers who did not come back to thank Jesus _____
9. A perfect number _____
10. Deuteronomy is book number _ in the Old Testament _____

1 The number of sheep who were lost out of the hundred _____
2 _____
3 _____
4 _____
5 _____
6 _____
7 _____
8 _____
9 _____
10 _____

Find the missing letters - 2

A CITY IS CAPTURED

Read Joshua 6 verses 2-5

Now fill in the instructions for Joshua
to tell his soldiers.

1. M__ch around the city o___ .
2. D_ th__ for ___ d___ .
3. S_v__ pr__sts carry tr_____ in
   front of the A__ .
4. Day s____ : M____ round the
   ____ s____ times, the p_____
   blowing the t_____ .
5. At the sound of a l___
   bl___, everybody s_____ .

Read the rest of the chapter and find out:

What had the people to shout? ____

_____

What happened when the people
gave the loud shout? _____

_____

MATCHING RELATIONS

Match the names of the couples on the left hand side to the correct relation- ship on the right hand side · · · · ·

Abraham & Lot	Brother/Sister
Ruth & Orpah	Mother/Daughter
Moses & Miriam	Mother/Son
Isaac & Joseph	Brothers
Lois & Eunice	Cousins
Joseph & Reuben	Uncle/Nephew
Mary & Elizabeth	Mother/Daughter-in-law
Eve & Seth	Grandfather/Grandson

Section 2

Perplexing Puzzles

WHO WAS THAT?

Who in the Bible do you think of when you see the following pictures?

1. A man up a tree looking for Jesus. _ _ _ _ _ _ _ _ _
2. Soldiers marching round the wall at Jericho. _ _ _ _ _ _ _
3. A blind man shouting : "Have mercy on me!" _ _ _ _ _ _ _ _ _
4. A young boy tells his older brothers about his dreams. _ _ _ _ _ _
5. A tax collector hears Jesus call "Follow me!" _ _ _ _ _ _ _
6. A young man plays a harp before King Saul. _ _ _ _ _
7. At Malta, this man shakes a viper off his hand into the fire. _ _ _ _ _
8. A man who gets caught in a tree by his hair. _ _ _ _ _ _ _ _

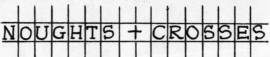

NOUGHTS + CROSSES

This game can be played in pairs or teams 'x' and 'o'.
Fill up the board as a correct answer is given.

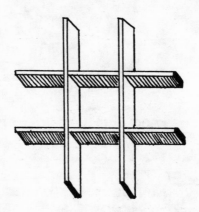

1. How many people were in the Ark?

2. How many lepers did Jesus heal?

3. How did Adam and Eve sin?

4. How did Stephen die?

5. Where did Martha, Mary and Lazarus live?

6. Where did Paul and Silas sing in prison?

7. Give the name of Moses' sister?

8. Give the name of Ruth's mother-in-law.

9. Name the man who prayed three times a day.

10. In whose tomb was Jesus buried?

The story of David crossword

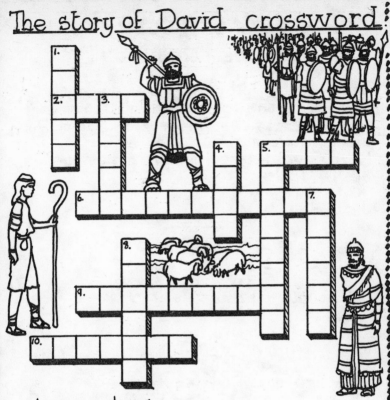

Across clues.

2. THE FIRST KING OF ISRAEL.
5. FOUGHT FOR DAVID.
6. ENEMIES OF THE ISRAELITES.
9. DAVID FELL IN LOVE WITH THIS PERSON.
10. A GIANT.

Down clues.

1. DAVID'S FATHER.
3. KILLED IN BATTLE.
4. DAVID FLED TO THIS PLACE.
5. DAVID'S CLOSEST FRIEND.
7. HE ANOINTED DAVID.
8. SENT BY GOD TO DAVID.

Can you CRACK the code?
What does this say?

Write out the letters of the alphabet.
Now give each letter a number, starting
with : A = 1, B = 2, C = 3 and so on
until you come to Z = 26.
Next, decode the following message which
Jesus spoke.

Jesus said :

"
20,1,11,5   3,15,21,18,1,7,5   9,20   9,19   9.
4,15,14'20   2,5   1,6,18,1,9,4."
                    (13,1,20,8,5,23, ch. 14, v. 27)

Write out what Jesus said here :

"____ _____! __ __ _. ___'_ __
_____.   (_____ ch. 14, v.27)

This time,
after writing
out the
alphabet
give A=26, B=25, C=24 and so until
you come to Z = 1.
The message below is a command from Jesus.

"
23,12   13,12,7   15,22,7   2,12,6,9   19,22,26,9,7,8
25,22   7,9,12,6,25,15 22,23. 7,9,6,8,7   18,13
20,12,23; 7,9,6,8,7   26,15,8,12   18,13   14,22"
                    (17,12,19,13 ch 14 v.1)

Write out the command below.

"
__ ___ ___ ____ _____ __
_____. ___.___ __ ___; _____
____ __ __." (____ ch. 14 v. 1)

TRUE OR FALSE?

PLAY THE FOLLOWING TWO GAMES··

Read the statements 1 - 9 below.
Decide whether they are true or false.

Put an 'X' for a true answer, or an 'O'
for a false answer against the
correct numbers in the diagram.

1. Luke was not one of the twelve disciples.
2. John the Baptist was beheaded.
3. There were eight plagues in Egypt.
4. The story of David and Goliath is found in Genesis.
5. Jonathan was David's best friend.
6. There are twenty seven books in the New Testament.
7. Honey was a food in Bible times.
8. Abel was a gardener.
9. Samuel's mother was Hannah.

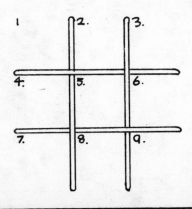

Name the Bible book

Give the name of the Bible book
from the clues below.

1. The first book in the Bible.

   _____

2. The last book in the Bible.

   _____

3. The story of David and Goliath
   is found here. _____

4. The shortest books in the Bible.

   _____

5. Shadrach, Meshach and Abednego's
   story is told in this book _____

6. Luke wrote this book _____

7. The Gospels

   _____

8. In this book we find the Ten
   Commandments. _____

Section 3

Quickie Quizzes

What is it?

READ THE DESCRIPTIONS BELOW AND
DECIDE WHAT EACH REFERS TO:

1. Jesus used this to feed 5,000 people.

2. Samson was told not to cut this.

3. Travellers in the time of Jesus liked this after a long journey.

4. David played this to please King Saul.

5. People were ordered to worship this by King Nebuchadnezzar.

6. Amos saw this in a vision from the Lord.

7. Fed to the children of Israel in the wilderness.

8. People dressed in this in Bible times to show that they were sorry for what they had done.

The Israelites v the Midianites.

Now read the following statements and after each one write whether it is true or false.

1.- GOD'S ANGEL APPEARED TO GIDEON WHEN HE WAS THRESHING WHEAT _____

2.- GIDEON WAS HAPPY TO SAVE THE ISRAELITES FROM THE MIDIANITES _____

3.- GOD PROMISED TO BE WITH GIDEON IN LEADING THE ISRAELITES _____

4.- GIDEON ASKED FOR SIGNS SO THAT HE WOULD KNOW GOD WOULD HELP HIM _____

5.- GIDEON'S FAMILY WAS PLEASED TO SEE BAAL'S ALTER DESTROYED _____

6.- GIDEON HAD TOO MANY MEN IN HIS ARMY _____

7.- THOSE WHO KNEELED TO DRINK WATER WERE ALLOWED TO STAY IN GIDEON'S ARMY _____

8.- THE THREE HUNDRED SOLDIERS CARRIED TORCHES, SHOUTING ' FOR THE LORD AND FOR GIDEON !' _____

9.- THE MIDIANITES WERE AFRAID AND FLED BEFORE THE ISRAELITE ARMY _____

Where did this take place?

WORK OUT THE ANSWERS FROM THE CLUES GIVEN

1. Elijah was fed here by ravens.
   _____

2. The Ark rested on this mountain.
   _____

3. The water did not taste sweet here.
   _____

4. Here the Israelites were defeated because they had stolen goods from this city _____

5. The Hebrews were sad here when they remembered how they used to worship God _____

6. At this place, a lame man was made to walk again and praised God _____

7. Paul preached here under guard
   _____

who am I?

Complete each name —

1. _____ the Baptist
2. _____ the dreamer
3. _____ the betrayer
4. _____ the harlot
5. _____ the Son of God
6. _____ the Moabitess
7. _____ the Psalmist
8. _____ the tax collector

Work out who I am from the clues.

9. A fisherman I used to be _____

10. An angel told me that I was to have a baby boy who would save people from their sins _____

11. A princess saw me in a basket boat _____

12. I was tempted to do wrong _____

13. I was maid to Sarah _____

14. My name means "to encourage" _____

15. I was told to preach to people who would not listen to me _____

16. I made Jacob work hard for me _____

PLACE THE PARABLES

Below are two parables in picture form. Put the pictures in the correct order by placing '1' beside the first picture and so on.

Parable 1 - The Lost Sheep

Parable 2 - The parable of the ten virgins.

Answer these
questions in the
space provided.

1. Why were Adam and Eve put out
of the Garden of Eden? _ _ _ _ _ _
_ _ _ _ _ _ _ _ _ _ _ _ _ _ _ _ _ _ _

2. Why did God send a flood on the Earth? _ _ _

3 Why did God tell Abraham to leave his
father's home? _ _ _ _ _ _ _ _ _ _ _

4. Why was Joseph put in charge of Pharaoh's
palace and the land of Egypt? _ _ _ _ _
_ _ _ _ _ _ _ _ _ _ _ _ _ _ _ _ _ _

5. Why did Haman ask King Xerxes to
sign a decree? _ _ _ _ _ _ _ _ _ _ _

6. Why did Peter weep after the cock
crowed? _ _ _ _ _ _ _ _ _ _ _ _ _

7. Why were different peoples able to hear
the sermon at Pentecost each in their
own language? _ _ _ _ _ _ _ _ _ _

8. Why did Paul land on the island of Malta?
_ _ _ _ _ _ _ _ _ _ _ _ _ _ _ _ _

Section 4

Ways With Words

JUMBLED BIBLE BOOKS.

UNJUMBLE THE FOLLOWING LETTERS TO MAKE BOOKS
IN THE BIBLE.

OLD TESTAMENT

DOEXSU

_ _ _ _ _ _

SKING

_ _ _ _ _

MOSA _ _ _ _

THRU _ _ _ _

HOJAN

_ _ _ _ _

SAPLSM

_ _ _ _ _ _

ANDLIE

_ _ _ _ _

RAEZ _ _ _ _

NEW TESTAMENT

OJHN _ _ _ _

TCAS _ _ _ _

ELKU _ _ _ _

SUTTI

_ _ _ _ _

MAJES

_ _ _ _ _

HILPMEON

_ _ _ _ _ _ _ _

SRMOAN

_ _ _ _ _ _

SWRHBEE

_ _ _ _ _ _ _

VERSE ENDINGS.

Choose the correct endings to the following verses. Put a line round your choice.

1. REMEMBER THE SABBATH DAY...
   1. BY KEEPING IT HOLY.
   2. BY READING THE BIBLE.
   3. BY RESTING.

2. FOR ALL HAVE SINNED .....
   1. AND FORGOTTEN GOD.
   2. AND FALLEN SHORT OF THE GLORY OF GOD.
   3. AND ARE FORGIVEN BY GOD.

3. TRUST IN THE LORD ••••
   1. WITH ALL YOUR HEART.
   2. AND YOU WILL FAVOUR WITH GOD.
   3. AND HE WILL DIRECT YOUR WAYS.

4. YOUR WORD IS A LAMP TO MY FEET ....
   1. GUIDING MY PATH.
   2. AND A LIGHT FOR MY PATH.
   3. AND A JOY OF MY HEART.

5. AND MY GOD WILL MEET ALL YOUR NEEDS.....
   1. AS HE HAS PROMISED.
   2. ACCORDING TO HIS GLORIOUS RICHES IN JESUS CHRIST.
   3. TO GOD BY THE GLORY FOR EVER AND EVER.

6. COMMIT YOUR WAY TO THE LORD ....
   1. AND HE WILL GIVE YOU THE DESIRES OF YOUR HEART.
   2. DO NOT FRET.
   3. TRUST IN HIM AND HE WILL DO THIS.

7. BLESSED ARE THE PURE IN HEART ....
   1. FOR THEY WILL SEE GOD.
   2. FOR THEY WILL BE CALLED THE SONS OF GOD.
   3. FOR THEY WILL BE FILLED.

8. YOU SHOULD NOT BE SURPRISED AT MY SAYING...
   1. GOD SO LOVED THE WORLD.
   2. YOU MUST BE BORN AGAIN.
   3. YOU CANNOT SEE THE KINGDOM OF GOD.

Missionary suitcase review.

Unjumble the letters in the words in this suitcase to find some of the places Paul visited during his missionary tours.

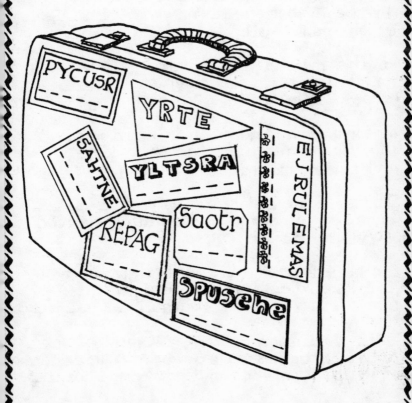

Find these places on a map.

Identify the Bible characters

WHO AM I?

SCORING:
* 3 POINTS FOR ANSWER IN (a)
* 2 POINTS FOR ANSWER IN (b)
* 1 POINT FOR ANSWER IN (c)

1 (a) He had twelve sons.
(b) He pretended to be his brother. _ _ _ _ _
(c) His favourite son was sold as a slave.

2 (a) She was the sister of Lazarus.
(b) She lived in Bethany. _ _ _ _ _ _
(c) She had a sister called Mary.

3 (a) This man's wife had a terrible dream.
(b) He was a Roman ruler. _ _ _ _ _ _
(c) Jesus appeared before him.

4 (a) He left his home with Abraham.
(b) Abraham was his uncle. _ _ _ _
(c) His wife turned into a pillar of salt.

5 (a) He led the children of Israel. _ _ _ _ _ _
(b) He was in charge of the fall of Jericho.
(c) A Bible Book is called after him.

6 (a) He was once called Belteshazzar.
(b) He would not eat the King's meat.
(c) He interpretted dreams. _ _ _ _ _ _

7 (a) He was a man sent from God. _ _ _ _
(b) He wore clothes made of camels hair. _ _ _
(c) He ate locusts and wild honey. _ _ _ _ _ _ _

8 (a) He brought back a widows son to life.
(b) He was fed by ravens. _ _ _ _ _ _
(c) He was lifted into heaven by a whirlwind.

BIBLE BOOK BEGINNINGS

Give the name of a Bible Book in the Old Testament beginning with:

A   R   P

L   D   J   M   O

Give the name of a New Testament Book beginning with:

E   T

J   P   M   R

A

H

JONAH

Tick the correct answers about Jonah.

1. Jonah was asked ......
   - to preach in Nineveh. ☐
   - to write a letter. ☐
   - to become a sailor. ☐

2. Jonah ......
   - did what God asked him. ☐
   - went aboard a ship. ☐
   - stayed at home. ☐

3. The storm at sea became calm after .....
   - the sailors returned home. ☐
   - Jonah was thrown overboard. ☐
   - they threw their cargo overboard. ☐

4. Jonah was inside the great fish for ......
   - one night. ☐
   - three days and three nights. ☐
   - one week. ☐

5. Jonah told the people of Nineveh ......
   - that God had forgiven them. ☐
   - to read their Bibles. ☐
   - 40 more days and Nineveh will be destroyed. ☐

6. The people ......
   - believed Jonah's message. ☐
   - killed Jonah. ☐
   - laughed at what Jonah had said. ☐

7. God ......
   - destroyed Nineveh. ☐
   - forgave the people of Nineveh. ☐
   - asked Jonah to preach to the people again. ☐

Mixed up Bible Book names.

Below are names of books in the Bible.
Unjumble the letters to find out what
they are.
Write the correct name below each
one in the diagram.

1. BOJ

_ _ _

2. DUJE

_ _ _ _

3. HAMIC

_ _ _ _ _

4. SHUJOA

_ _ _ _ _ _

5. WMATTEH

_ _ _ _ _ _ _

6. PHESIANSE

_ _ _ _ _ _ _ _ _

7. LOJE

_ _ _ _

8. REPTE

_ _ _ _ _

9. GESDJU

_ _ _ _ _ _

BIBLE EVENTS IN PICTURES.
What do the pictures tell us?

IDENTIFY THE FOLLOWING BIBLE EVENTS FROM THE SKETCHES BELOW.

___ The parable of the Sower.
___ David and Goliath.
___ The Lost Coin.
___ Moses and the Burning Bush.
___ Paul on the way to Damascus.
___ Jonah preaches to the people of Nineveh.

Section 5

Who's Who
and
What's What?

Old or New Testament Events.

Decide in which part of the Bible these events take place and write "Old Testament" or "New Testament" after each one.

1. THE PLAGUES OF EGYPT.

   ___ _____

2. THE BUILDING OF THE TOWER OF BABEL.

   ___ _____

3. THE FALL OF JERICHO.

4. THE STONING OF STEPHEN.

   ___ _____

5. LAZARUS IS RAISED FROM THE DEAD.

   ___ _____

6. BELSHAZZAR SAW WRITING ON THE WALL.

   ___

7. A RULER'S WIFE HAD A FEARFUL DREAM.

   ___ _____

8. JOHN WRITES LETTERS TO SEVEN CHURCHES.

   ___ _____

Who made these headlines in the Old Testament?

1. **M**an builds ark on dry ground.

   _ _ _ _

2. **P**LAGUES IN EGYPT.

   _ _ _ _ _ _ _ _

3. **Y**oung man kills giant..!

   _ _ _ _

4. **M**AN IS FED BY BIRDS!

   _ _ _ _ _

5. **Q**ueen visits palace.

   _ _ _ _ _ _ _ _ _ _ _ _

6. **P**ROPHET IS THROWN INTO A DUNGEON !

   _ _ _ _ _ _ _

7. **T**hree men kept alive in a blazing furnace.

   _ _ _ _ _ _ _ _   _ _ _ _ _ _

   _ _ _ _ _   _ _ _ _

8. **R**UNAWAY SPENDS THREE DAYS IN A LARGE FISH   _ _ _ _ _

WHO SAID THIS?

1. "The serpent deceived me and I ate."

_ _ _

2. "God will provide the lamb for the burnt offering, my son."

_ _ _ _ _ _ _

3. "Your servants have come to buy food."

_ _ _ _ _ _ ' _ _ _ _ _ _ _

4. "I am who I am." _ _ _

5. "I know that my Redeemer lives."

_ _ _

6. "Feed my sheep." _ _ _ _ _

7. "Rejoice in the Lord always." _ _ _ _

8. "Sirs, what must I do to be saved?"

_ _ _ _ _ _ _ _ _ _ _ _ _ _ _ _ _

MADE ? BY

1. A BRASS SERPENT.
_ _ _ _ _

2. A MOLTEN CALF.
_ _ _ _ _

3. APRONS OF LEAVES.
_ _ _ _   _ _ _   _ _ _

4. GALLOWS TO HANG MORDECAI.
_ _ _ _ _

5. AN ARK OF BULRUSHES.
_ _ _ _ _   _ _ _ _ _ _

6. MEAL FOR 5,000 PEOPLE.
_ _ _ _ _

7. A COAT OF MANY COLOURS.
_ _ _ _ _

8. A SUPPER FOR JESUS IN BETHANY.
_ _ _ _ _

SPOT THE MISTAKE

Cross out the wrong word and write the correct word above.

DANIEL IN THE DEN OF LIONS, DANIEL, 6.

King Nebuchadnezzar had made Daniel rule over his kingdom. Men had become jealous of the King. They asked Daniel to sign a law forbidding anyone to pray to God. If anybody did pray during thirty days, they would be made a ruler. Daniel continued to pray to God three times a day. This was reported to the King. King Cyrus was pleased about this and so Daniel was thrown into the lions' den. The King could not sleep that night and had to get up to see if Daniel was alive. He shouted "Have your friends rescued you?" Daniel replied "God sent his angel to shut the lions' mouths!" The King was glad but left Daniel in the den. The King ordered that the lions had to be killed.

Who made these headlines in the New Testament?

1. **A**NGELS APPEAR AS MEN WATCH THEIR SHEEP.
_____

2. **M**AN CLIMBS TREE TO SEE JESUS.
_____

3. **Y**OUNG GIRL IS HEALED BY JESUS!
_____

4. **W**OMAN DISCOVERS AN EMPTY TOMB.
_____

5. **A** VIOLENT WIND FILLS A WHOLE HOUSE.
_____

6. **A** RIOT TAKES PLACE IN EPHESUS.
_____

7. **K**ING ALMOST PERSUADED TO BE A CHRISTIAN. _____

8. **M**EN SING AND PRAY TO GOD IN PRISON!
_____

Section 6

Choosing Correctly

Odd Bod

Identify which word does not belong in each list. Underline the odd one out.

1. Myrrh, Frankincense, silver, gold.

2. Peter, John, Luke, Matthew.

3. Saul, Solomon, David, Samuel.

4. Corinth, Rome, Philippi, Jerusalem, Ephesus.

5. Rachel, Miriam, Ruth, Sarah, Esther.

6. Elijah, Hosea, Joel, Amos, Jeremiah.

7. Daniel, Noah, Nebuchadnezzar, Cyrus, Abednego.

8. Silas, Paul, Timothy, Barnabas, Lazarus.

ABOUT JOSEPH·····

Underline the correct
answer in the
sentences about
Joseph.

1. Joseph's father gave
him ··· A RING / A
LONG COAT / GOLD.

2. Joseph's brothers were feeding their
flocks at ··· DOTHAN / EGYPT / BETHEL.

3. Joseph was sold for ··· 30 / 50 / 20
PIECES OF SILVER.

4. Pharoah saw ··· SEVEN COWS / CAMELS /
SHEEP IN ONE OF HIS DREAMS.

5. Joseph's brothers came to Egypt to···
SEE JOSEPH / TO BUY FOOD / TO VISIT THE KING.

6. Joseph's cup was hidden in ··· REUBEN'S /
BENJAMIN'S / HIS SERVANT'S SACK.

7. Joseph was successful because ··· HE WAS
CLEVER / TRUSTED GOD / OWNED MUCH LAND.

8. Joseph died at the age of ···
110 / 100 / 98 YEARS.

HIDDEN BOOKS.

The name of ten Bible books are hidden in the following sentences.
Underline them as you find them.
Number 1 is done for you·····

1. The <u>Johns</u>on family has gone away on holiday.

2. I have to travel six miles to my job every day.

3. The teacher remarked on how well the class listened to the story.

4. I read a most interesting book about garden flowers.

5. Acts of necessity and mercy are allowed on the Sabbath day.

6. The birds nest here every year.

7. In Revelation we read:
"because you are lukewarm, neither hot nor cold, I am about to spit you out of my mouth."

8. He tripped over the rut, hurting his leg as he fell.

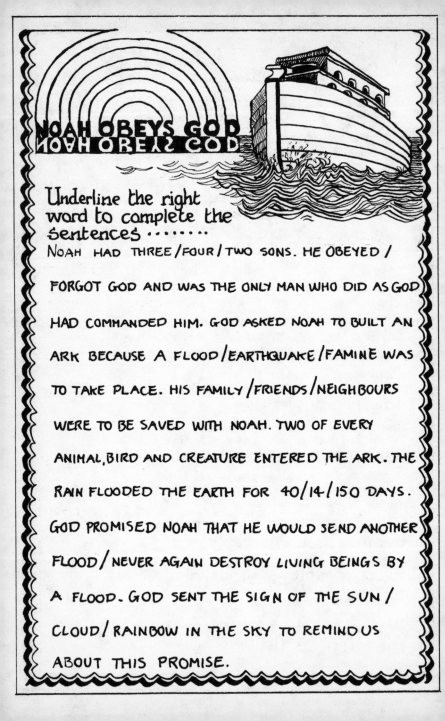

NOAH OBEYS GOD
NOAH OBEYS GOD

Underline the right
word to complete the
sentences ·······

NOAH HAD THREE / FOUR / TWO SONS. HE OBEYED /

FORGOT GOD AND WAS THE ONLY MAN WHO DID AS GOD

HAD COMMANDED HIM. GOD ASKED NOAH TO BUILT AN

ARK BECAUSE A FLOOD / EARTHQUAKE / FAMINE WAS

TO TAKE PLACE. HIS FAMILY / FRIENDS / NEIGHBOURS

WERE TO BE SAVED WITH NOAH. TWO OF EVERY

ANIMAL, BIRD AND CREATURE ENTERED THE ARK. THE

RAIN FLOODED THE EARTH FOR 40 / 14 / 150 DAYS.

GOD PROMISED NOAH THAT HE WOULD SEND ANOTHER

FLOOD / NEVER AGAIN DESTROY LIVING BEINGS BY

A FLOOD. GOD SENT THE SIGN OF THE SUN /

CLOUD / RAINBOW IN THE SKY TO REMIND US

ABOUT THIS PROMISE.

MEN AND WOMEN OF THE BIBLE

Underline the correct name in the following sentences...

1. HEROD / PILATE / PHAROAH TALKED TO THE WISE MEN.

2. MOSES / DAVID / JOSEPH WROTE THE 23rd PSALM.

3. PAUL AND PETER / JOHN / SILAS WERE HAPPY IN PRISON TOGETHER.

4. RAHAB / MARY / SARAH HID THE SPIES SENT TO JERICHO.

5. RHODA / NAOMI / LEAH ANSWERED PETER'S KNOCK AT THE DOOR.

6. EVE / REBEKAH / QUEEN OF SHEBA CAME TO VISIT KING SOLOMON.

7. JETHRO / JOAB / ELI WAS FATHER-IN-LAW OF MOSES.

8. DORCAS / ELIZABETH / RACHEL WAS GOOD AT NEEDLEWORK.

ANSWERS

Section 1 — A Mixture of Matching

1. MATCHING: Solomon–King; Elisha–Prophet; Eve-First Woman; Peter–Disciple; Vashti–Queen; Nicodemus–Ruler; Caleb–Spy; Adam–First Man; Potiphar–Soldier.

2. BIBLE PEOPLE WHO BELONG TOGETHER: Scribes and Pharisees; Martha and Mary; Ananias and Sapphira; Aquila and Priscilla; Sodom and Gomorrah; David and Jonathan.

3. FIND THE MISSING LETTERS: 1) A storm is calmed.
   COMPLETED WORDS: Jesus; disciples; people; strong; wind; waves; boat; afraid; asleep; Teacher; drown; still; calm.

4. PICTURE WORDS — Completed verse: Dear children. Keep yourselves from idols. *1 John 5 v. 21*.

5. MATCH THE BROTHERS: Abel and Cain; Andrew and Peter; Esau and Jacob; Benjamin and Joseph; Aaron and Moses; James and John; Dan and Naphtali; Shem and Japheth.

6. IN THE RIGHT ORDER — Correct Numbers: 1) 4 2) 3 3) 1 4) 6 5) 8 6) 10 7) 2 8) 9 9) 7 10) 5.
   Correct order: 1) No. 3 2) No. 7 3) No. 2 4) No. 1 5) No. 10 6) No. 4 7) No. 9 8) No. 5 9) No. 8 10) No. 6.

7. FIND THE MISSING LETTERS: 2) A city is captured.
   COMPLETED WORDS: 1) March; once 2) Do; this; six; days 3) Seven; priests; trumpets; ark 4) Seven; March; city; seven; priests; trumpets 5) Loud; blast; shout.

8. MATCHING RELATIONS: Ruth/Orpah–
Mother/Daughter-in-law; Moses/Miriam –
Brother/Sister; Isaac/Joseph – Grandfather/
Grandson; Lois/Eunice – Mother/Daughter;
Joseph/Reuben –Brothers; Mary/Elizabeth –
Cousins; Eve/Seth – Mother/Son.

Section 2 — Perplexing Puzzles

1. WHO WAS THAT: 1) Zacchaeus 2) Joshua 3)
Bartimeus 4) Joseph 5) Matthew 6) David 7) Paul
8) Absalom.

2. NOUGHTS AND CROSSES: 1) eight 2) ten 3)
they ate the forbidden fruit 4) he was stoned to
death 5) Bethany 6) Philippi 7) Miriam 8) Naomi
9) Daniel 10) Joseph of Arimathaea.

3. STORY OF DAVID CROSSWORD: Across clues
— 2) Saul 5) Joab 6) Philistines 9) Bathsheba 10)
Goliath. Down clues — 1) Jesse 3) Uriah 4) Gath
5) Jonathan 7) Samuel 8) Nathan.

4. CAN YOU CRACK THE CODE?
   Message 1—Take courage! It is I. Don't be
afraid. *Matthew 14, v. 27*
   Message 2 — Do not let your hearts be
troubled. Trust in God; trust also in Me. *John 14,
v. 1*.

5. TRUE OR FALSE? 1)True 2) True 3) False 4)
False 5) True 6) True 7) True 8) False 9) True.

6. NAME THE BIBLE BOOK: 1) Genesis 2) Revela-
tion 3) First Samuel 4) Second and Third John 5)
Daniel 6) Acts 7) Matthew, Mark Luke, John 8)
Exodus.

Section 3 — Quickie Quizzes

1. WHAT IS IT?: 1) small loaves 2) hair 3) Water 4)
harp 5) idol 6) plumbline 7) manna/quails 8)
sackcloth.

2. THE ISRAELITES v. THE MIDIANITES:
1) True 2) False 3) True 4) True 5) False; 6) True
7) False 8) True 9) True.

3. WHERE DID THIS TAKE PLACE?: 1) Kerith 2)
Ararat 3) Meribah 4) Ai 5) Babylon 6) At the
Gate Beautiful 7) Rome.

4. WHO AM I?: 1) John 2) Joseph 3) Judas
4) Rahab 5) Jesus 6) Ruth 7) David 8) Matthew 9)
Peter 10) Mary 11) Moses 12) Eve
13) Hagar 14) Barnabas 15) Isaiah 16) Laban.

5. PLACE THE PARABLES —
   THE LOST SHEEP: Correct order — picture 2;
   picture 3; picture 1; picture 4.
   THE TEN VIRGINS: Correct order —picture 4;
   picture 1; picture 3; picture 2.

6. WHY?
   1) They ate of the tree of the knowledge of
      Good and Evil.
   2) He was angry at the people's sin.
   3) He was going to bless him and make him
      into a great nation.
   4) The Lord was with Joseph in all that he
      did and Pharaoh had chosen him as the
      wisest man in Egypt.
   5) In order to kill the Jewish nation.
   6) He remembered what Jesus had said to
      him.
   7) The Holy Spirit helped the apostles to
      speak in different languages.
   8) His boat was shipwrecked.

Section 4 — Ways with Words

1. JUMBLED BIBLE BOOKS
      O.T. Exodus; Kings; Amos; Ruth; Jonah; Psalms; Daniel; Ezra.
      N.T. John; Acts; Luke; Titus; James; Philemon; Romans; Hebrews.

2. VERSE ENDINGS — 1) 1 2) 2 3) 3 4) 2 5) 2 6) 1 7) 1 8) 2.

3. MISSIONARY SUITCASE REVIEW— Cyprus; Tyre; Jerusalem; Athens; Lystra; Ephesus; Perga; Troas.

4. IDENTIFY THE BIBLE CHARACTERS — 1) Jacob 2) Martha 3) Pilate 4) Lot 5) Joshua 6) Daniel 7) John The Baptist 8) Elijah.

5. BIBLE BOOK BEGINNINGS —
O.T. Amos; Psalms; Obadiah; Ruth; Daniel; Leviticus/Lamentations; Ecclesiastes; Jeremiah.
N.T. Acts; Peter/Philippians; Ephesians; Hebrews; Titus/Timothy; Matthew; Luke; Revelation.

6. TICK THE CORRECT ANSWERS ABOUT JONAH —
      1) To preach in Nineveh.
      2) went aboard a ship.
      3) Jonah was thrown overboard.
      4) three days and three nights.
      5) 40 more days and Nineveh will be destroyed.
      6) The people of Nineveh believed Jonah's message.
      7) God forgave the people of Nineveh.

7. MIXED UP BIBLE BOOK NAMES — Job; Jude; Micah; Joshua; Matthew; Ephesians; Joel; Peter; Judges.

8   BIBLE EVENTS IN PICTURES — Correct order:
   1) Moses and the burning bush.
   2) David and Goliath.
   3) Jonah preaches to the people of Nineveh.
   4) The Parable of the Sower.
   5) Paul on the way to Damascus.
   6) The Lost Coin.

Section 5 — Who's Who and What's What?

1. OLD OR NEW TESTAMENT EVENTS? — 1) Old Testament 2) Old Testament 3) Old Testament 4) New Testament 5) New Testament 6) Old Testament 7) New Testament 8) New Testament.

2. WHO MADE THE HEADLINES IN THE OLD TESTAMENT? — 1) Noah 2) Israelites 3) David 4) Elijah 5) Queen of Sheba 6) Jeremiah 7) Shadrach; Meshach; Abednego 8) Jonah.

3. WHO SAID THIS? — 1) Eve 2) Abraham 3) Joseph's brothers 4) God 5) Job 6) Jesus 7) Paul 8) The Philippian jailer.

4. MADE BY? — 1) Moses 2) Aaron 3) Adam and Eve 4) Haman 5) Moses' mother 6) Jesus 7) Jacob 8) Martha.

5. SPOT THE MISTAKES? (wrong word followed by correct word) —

   Line 1 — Nebuchadnezzar (Cyrus).
   Line 3 — King (Daniel).
   Line 4 — Daniel (the King).
   Line 7 — a ruler (put into the lion's den).

Line 9 — pleased (sad).

Line 12 — Have your friends rescued you? (Has your God been able to save you?).

Line 15 — left Daniel in the den (Daniel was taken out of the den).

Line 16 — the king ordered that the lions had to be killed (the men who falsely accused Daniel were thrown into the lion's den).

6. WHO MADE THESE HEADLINES IN THE NEW TESTAMENT? —
    1) The shepherds.
    2) Zacchaeus.
    3) Jairus' daughter; Mary Magdalene.
    4) Holy Spirit comes at Pentecost.
    5) Paul opposed the idolatry in Ephesus and a riot resulted.
    6) King Agrippa.
    7) Paul and Silas in prison.

Section 6 — Choosing correctly

1. ODD BOD — silver; Peter; Samuel; Jerusalem; Ruth; Elijah; Noah; Lazarus.

2. ABOUT JOSEPH — a long coat; Dothan; 20; seven cows; to buy food; Benjamin's sack; he trusted God; 110.

3. HIDDEN BOOKS — John; Job; Mark; Amos; Acts; Esther; Luke; Ruth.

4. NOAH OBEYS GOD — three sons; obeyed; flood; family; 40 days; never again destroy living beings by a flood; rainbow.

5. MEN AND WOMEN OF THE BIBLE — Herod; David; Paul and Silas; Rahab; Rhoda; Queen of Sheba; Jethro; Dorcas.